get this
party
started!

get this
party
started!

50 NAUGHTY GAMES

for ❖ twosomes, ❖❖ threesomes, ❖❖ foursomes, and more

by FRANCES HILL • illustrations by DAN SIPPLE

CHRONICLE BOOKS
SAN FRANCISCO

Text copyright © 2006 by Frances Hill.
Illustrations copyright © 2006 by Dan Sipple.
All rights reserved. No part of this book may be reproduced
in any form without written permission from the publisher.

Library of Congress Cataloging-in-Publication Data available.

ISBN: 0-8118-4870-1

Manufactured in Hong Kong

Designed by Headcase Design

Distributed in Canada by Raincoast Books
9050 Shaughnessy Street
Vancouver, British Columbia V6P 6E5

10 9 8 7 6 5 4 3 2 1

Chronicle Books LLC
85 Second Street
San Francisco, California 94105

www.chroniclebooks.com

Scrabble is a registered trademark of Hasbro, Inc.
Twister is a registered trademark of Milton Bradley.
Trademark owners do not sponsor, endorse,
or support the games in *Get This Party Started!*

contents

Hot Stuff 42

Raunchy 68

Hardcore 90

Appendix

INTRODUCTION

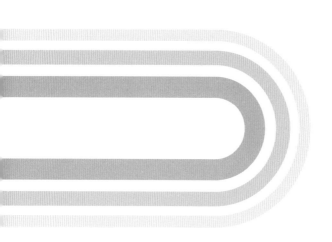

FEELING NAUGHTY?

Then you've come to the right place. *Get This Party Started!* features fifty games custom-made for your inner bad child.

Remember that hot adrenaline rush you felt as a kid when you got caught doing something naughty—like sneaking away to play Spin the Bottle, French kissing on the sofa, or groping in the backseat of the car? Remember how the risk of being caught in the act made it even more titillating? (Maybe you even secretly hoped for a good spanking.) Well, now that you're an adult, you can recapture that same electric thrill by playing the games in *Get This Party Started!* We've taken classics you'll remember from childhood—such as Hide and Seek, Marco Polo, and Scrabble—and tweaked the rules to make them a little (or a lot) more naughty and definitely more fun. We've also created original games that are sure to score big points with your friends and lovers.

Here you'll find sexy games for everyone—both nervous Nellies and goodtime Charlies. To make things easy, we've organized the games into chapters according to the level of naughtiness. Chapter 1, "Virginal," has saucy games that will leave you blushing but (mostly) untouched, while chapter 4, "Hardcore," features more daring encounters you will blush to remember. You'll find games for twosomes, threesomes, foursomes, and more. Some games require props (these are noted below the heading of each game), but most can be played with just a few willing adults and a sense of adventure.

The beauty of these games is that it doesn't really matter if you win or lose. No matter what, secret desires will be revealed and players will inevitably be spanked, stripped, kissed, or fondled along the way. Leave the book on your coffee table for friends to flip through, dog-ear your favorite game and leave it under your partner's pillow as a hint, or copy one and send it out with an invitation to friends to come over and play next Saturday night. They'll soon find out that being a little bit bad can be very, very good.

Let the naughty games begin!

THE RATING/ METER

VIRGINAL: You can leave your hat on, as well as your clothes. These games feature mostly dirty words and thoughts, with a few opportunities to reach first base.

HOT STUFF: Requires necking, touching, or partial nudity. Body heat is sure to rise.

RAUNCHY: You'll be forced to remove some or all of your clothes, and spanking, fondling, or nude body contact is likely.

HARDCORE: Highly erotic or sexual acts involved!

NAUGHTY NAME/

Giving yourself a new name makes it easier to become someone else for an hour or two. And it's easy! Choose a sexy confection like Ginger or Sugar or Rod, or try a play on words like Madame Ovary or Trojan Boy. The classic way to create a naughty "porn star" name is to take the name of a pet for your first name and match it to the name of the street you grew up on. Play with your choices till the name sounds just right, perhaps Lucky Lane, Brandy Rodeo, Honey Bohemia, or Max Washington.

WHO ARE YOU?

Remember when you played dress up with your parent's clothes and pretended to be all grown up? To get in the spirit of *these* games, choose a naughty persona and dress for it. Will you be the passive one or the aggressor? Doctor or patient, dominatrix or slave, headmistress or naughty schoolboy? Or will you simply cross-dress to see how it feels? If you're hosting a naughty party, you can encourage "dress-up" by providing costumes, accessories, body paint, and hats for everyone to choose from and wear.

virg

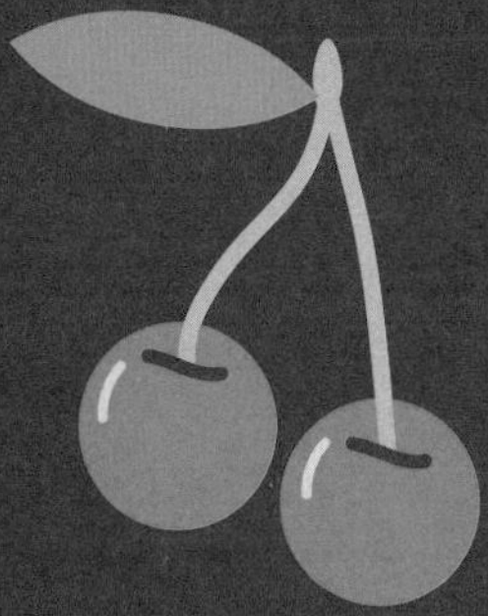

inal

PROPS:
Pen, paper, paper bags, and a timer.

PLAYERS:
Foursome (not including host) or more

Are those trashy supermarket tabloids one of your guilty pleasures? Don't be ashamed—put all that useless trivia to work. Here's a guessing game where you can flaunt your knowledge of celebrities' sins and win!

 In advance, the host should write down on individual pieces of paper the names of fifty celebrities, dead or alive, who are notorious for their sexual escapades or lifestyle. Place them in a paper sack.

 Split into two teams. On each team, one is the clue-giver, and the other(s) guess. Each team has sixty seconds to see how many celebrities they can guess.

 The host starts the timer and the first team's clue-giver pulls a slip of paper from the sack. As quickly as he or she can, the clue-giver offers as many hints or clues about the celebrity as possible without saying the person's name. For example: for Kobe Bryant, the clues could be LA Lakers player, Colorado hotel room; for Marilyn Monroe, "Happy birthday, Mr. President," *Some Like It Hot*, famous *Playboy* photo.

sack?

 4

As soon as the team guesses correctly, the clue-giver pulls another name out of the sack, and so on until time is up. Then the sack is passed to the other team, who repeats the process. The game continues, with each team getting a turn to guess, until the sack is empty. The team with the most slips of paper on its side wins.

Note: Suggested candidates for misbehaving celebrities: Jenna Jameson, Hugh Grant, Cary Grant, Bill Clinton, Howard Stern, Fatty Arbuckle, Josephine Baker, Madonna, Janet Jackson, Michael Jackson, Caligula, Ron Jeremy.

bobbing

PROPS:
Martinis in martini glasses, olives, and two small bowls

PLAYERS:
Six players or more

Sure, bobbing for apples was fun when you were a kid, but now that you're all grown up, you may be surprised at how much more fun the game can be when played with cocktails and olives.

① Break into two equal teams. Serve martinis—gin or vodka, your choice—one for each member of each team. Place one olive in each drink, and the drinks on a table. Place a bowl by each team's drinks.

② Each team stands in a line. The first player in each line bobs for an olive in a martini glass. He or she must whisk it out with mouth and teeth only, and then must pass it to the next player in line. The olive must be passed back until it is in the mouth of the last person in line.

③ That person must then run to the front of the line, spit the olive into the bowl, and bob for the fresh olive in the next martini. The olive is passed back by mouth in the same fashion, until it reaches the last person in line, who runs to the front.

④ The first team to get their starting person back to the front of the line wins.

VIRGINAL

for olives

king of the

PROPS:
Large vinyl or plastic sheet to form the wrestling mat, tape (optional), and body oil

PLAYERS:
Threesome or more

Remember playing King of the Mountain in the sandbox? Now you can test your skills with the help of some slithery oil. Feel free to blast the eponymous song by Bon Jovi for inspiration.

1   Place a vinyl or plastic sheet on the surface to be wrestled on. We recommend the floor, but a bed will do, too. You may want to tape it down.

2   All guests should wear snug-fitting trunks or bathing suits, and oil yourselves until your bodies glisten.

3   At the count of three, jump onto the mat from different corners and wrestle, tickle, push, and pull to force your opponents off the mat. Your aim is to remain standing as King of the Mountain. Once someone falls off the mat, even by a big toe, he or she is out.

4   The losers must massage the King (or Queen). And you thought the oil was just for wrestling?

mountain

i never

PROPS:	PLAYERS:
Ten packaged condoms for each player	Foursome or more

Ever wonder if everybody else is doing things you've always longed to try but never have? Now you can find out!

 Each player begins with ten condoms. These are the chips for the game.

 One player begins by saying "I never..." and fills in the blank with something sexual she or he has never done. This can be almost anything except for patently absurd activities no one could or would do. For example, a player might say, "I never slept with someone who was married," "I never took it up the ass," "I never did it with another girl," or "I never flirted with my boss." Saying, "I never did it with a deer" or "I never did it in space" doesn't count. Anyone around the table who has done the act must put a condom in the middle of the table.

 The next player then makes an "I never" statement, and it keeps going around the table, one turn each. The first person to get rid of all her or his condoms wins and gets to keep the entire stash.

orange

This game was played, hilariously, in a French nightclub scene in the stylish Audrey Hepburn and Cary Grant film *Charade*. Players come in extremely close contact with one another, so snug-fitting clothing is advised. In this version, we've added handcuffs for a naughtier edge.

 Divide into two teams of equal number, each forming a line.

 Choose one person to be the Orangemeister, who will handcuff or tie team members' hands behind their backs.

 The Orangemeister tucks an orange beneath the chin of the first person in line on each team.

 That player must pass the orange, chin-to-chin, to the next person in line, who must pass the orange to the next player, and so on down the line.

 If the orange drops, the Orangemeister replaces the orange under the player's chin and the couple starts again.

 If the line is long, the game ends when the orange is under the chin of the last person in line. If the teams are small, the game can be prolonged by having the last person in line bring the orange to the front of the line, and the orange is

meister

passed back again. In this case, the first team to get their original starting person back to the front wins. Winning teams are released from bondage by the Orangemeister, but the losing team can only be uncuffed by a winning team member, which could lead to a different kind of game playing.

key chain

PROP∫:
Two large keys, string

PLAYER∫:
Six players or more

This game is an excellent excuse to get underneath someone else's clothes.

❶ Several hours before the game is played, tie two keys each with their own very long piece of string (at least fifty feet) and place them in the freezer. Very large, old-fashioned keys are best (look in second-hand shops).

❷ Players should divide into two teams of equal number, each forming a line. The first person in line on each team holds the cold key with attached string.

❸ On a set signal, the game begins. Each team member threads the key down the front of the clothes of the person next in line, as quickly as possible. The key must touch skin all the way down, going under or inside shirts, skirts, pants, bras, underwear, and so on until the key hits the floor. The person being "keyed" cannot touch the key or assist in any way.

❹ The "keyed" player picks up the key and threads the person next in line in the same fashion, while the person who was first in line now goes to the end of the line and will be the last to be threaded. The first team to be totally threaded together wins.

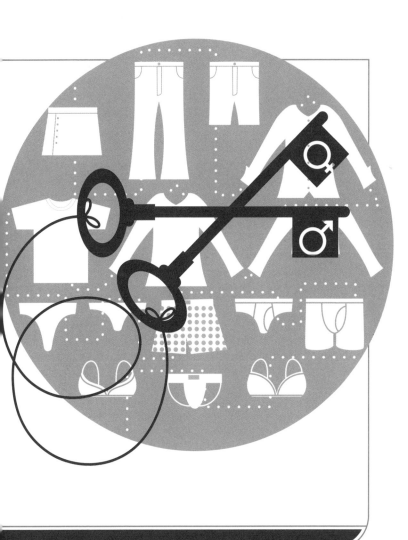

lucky

PROPS:
Blindfold, martinis (optional)

PLAYERS:
Foursome, but preferably more

This game will have you lap dancing blindfolded. You'll have no idea whose lap you're in until you start wiggling. So get dancing, duck! We recommend martinis to kick off this game and as the method of choosing the first duck.

 Prepare a round of martinis for all players. Place a green olive in each glass except for one, which gets a black olive.

 The host gives the martini with the black olive to whomever he or she wishes to be the first "Dancing Duck."

 After drinks are consumed, everyone sits cross-legged in a circle.

 The black olive holder now stands, is blindfolded, and turned by the host three times in the middle of the circle. The blindfolded player must now crawl in any direction. He or she must climb into the lap of the first person he or she reaches and guess who it is. Wiggling and rubbing up against the body is allowed, but not using your hands.

 The lap dancer may ask only one question: "Lucky Ducky?" And "the lap" may only respond "Quack quack." The question may be repeated as many times as the Dancing Duck wishes.

ducky

6 When the Dancing Duck thinks he or she can guess the identity of the lap, the person calls out the name. If correct, the blindfold is removed, and the player who was the lap becomes the next lap dancer. If the Dancing Duck guesses incorrectly, the circle all quacks and the wiggling resumes until the lap's identity is guessed correctly.

high ball

PROPS:
Rubber balls of varying colors or patterns, two of each; one or two bowls

PLAYERS:
Foursome, but preferably more

If two people like the same color, perhaps they have more in common that should be explored? This game will help you find out.

1 Fill a large bowl with small rubber balls of varying colors or patterns. There should be two of each kind, and one for each guest. Ask each guest to choose a ball. If you want to ensure male-female couples, split each pair of patterned balls between two bowls, and have the men pick from one and the women from the other.

2 Pair guests off by couples who have chosen identical balls. Only one ball will now be needed per couple to play the game.

3 Each couple stands face to face, holding one ball between their bellies.

4 The object is to roll the ball, using rotary movements of the body only—no hands—up to one person's chin (usually the shorter of the two).

5 On a set signal, the game begins, and the first pair to get their ball tucked beneath a chin wins.

newlybeds

PROPS:	PLAYERS:
Pen and paper	Two couples (not including emcee) or more

A spoof on *The Newlywed Game*, this is best played by couples who've been together a while—and think they know each other.

 Make two groups by splitting each couple and putting them in different groups. One person or one couple plays the emcee. One group stays in the same room with the emcee; the other group goes to another room where they can't hear the first group, preferably in the kitchen making blender drinks.

 The emcee writes down a series of intimate sexual questions (this can be done in advance), and asks each person in the first group to answer them. Suggestions: What is your favorite position? How often does your partner initiate sex? What do you wear to bed? The answer for each person should be written down.

 The second group is invited back (bringing in a round of drinks for all), and each couple is reunited and sits together. The emcee asks members of the second group to guess how their partner answered each question. Take each question in turn until all couples have answered it. One point is awarded for each correct answer, and the highest scoring couple wins.

most likely

PROPS:	PLAYERS:
Paper and pen	Threesome or more

High school yearbooks highlighted those students most likely to succeed in careers, but what about those most likely to succeed in the bedroom? This game will help you find out what your friends really think about your sex life.

 The host alone or the group (individually and in secret) writes down about fifteen categories in total. The categories should be subjective qualities, such as Best Girl/Boy in Bed, Sluttiest, Hottest, Most Likely to Sleep with the Football Team, Quietest Lay, Most Likely to Star in a Porn Film, and so on.

 The host reads or lists each question, and everyone votes by secret ballot who they think should "win" each category.

  The host tallies the anonymous votes for each category out loud, and on a large piece of paper (your sex yearbook) lists the winners.

Most likely to...

hot ru

PROPS:	PLAYERS:
None	Foursome, preferably more

Inspired by the game Gossip, these rumors are hot and coming faster than a fifteen-year-old boy. *What* did you say!?

① Ask guests to sit in a circle close enough to each other so they can whisper in their neighbor's ear.

② The host starts an X-rated rumor by whispering in the person's ear to the left as quickly as possible, without repeating the rumor. For mischievous fun, include the name of one of the players in the rumor. Each person whispers to the next, and so on, until the rumor gets to the last person, who blurts out what she or he heard.

③ If the phrase reaches the end of the circle the same as the way it started, the person who announced it is docked a point. If beautifully muddled, the originator scores 2 points. A new rumor is passed around, this time initiated by the person to the left of the previous rumormonger.

④ The first person to score 6 points wins.

drawing

PROPS:	PLAYERS:
Paper and pen for each player, one six-sided die	Foursome or more

Michelangelo's masterpiece *David* is probably the most famous sculpture in the world, and oh so erotic. But can you draw that contrapposto, or create an even better pose? The luck of the roll will decide if you can.

Each player rolls the die, and the one rolling the highest number gets to select a player who will be the model for this life drawing class. The high roller may pose the model as he or she chooses (clothes remain on—though you can be as exhibitionist as you want to be), offering everyone a suitably sexy subject to sketch. All drawings, however, should be like *David*—in the nude.

Proceed clockwise around the table, each player choosing a guest to model and arranging the pose.

After each player has had a turn, pin up the drawings and all vote on which is the hottest piece of art.

VIRGINAL

pin the

PROPS:
Blindfold, a sexy centerfold pinup, a cut-out paper penis for each player, push pins, and paper and pens

PLAYERS:
Threesome or more

Betcha tried pinning the tail on the donkey at a birthday party when you were little. Now try nailing something a little more grown-up.

 Tape a nude male or female centerfold to the wall or door.

 Ask each guest to write down on a piece of paper the place he or she most craves either to penetrate or be penetrated. Each player should put his or her name on the paper and hand the paper over to the host.

 Hand each player a cutout of a generous penis with his or her name written on it and a push pin attached. Blindfold one player at a time. Spin the player around, and point the person in the direction of the glorious pinup. The player must try to stick the penis on the spot he or she wrote down.

 After all players have had their turn, the host reads the papers telling where guests' cravings lie . . . was it really a tale of wanting it in the ear, or was that misguided?

 The player who pins the penis closest to the spot he or she wrote down wins.

VIRGINAL

pinup

who do you think you are?

The perfect icebreaker, this game forces guests to talk about themselves, only they don't know who they really are.

Prior to the party, the host writes or draws a body part on pieces of paper, making sure there is one for each player.

As each player arrives, the host offers a cocktail and pins a paper to his or her back without letting the player read it. Players can see the signs on other backs, just not their own.

Players must discover who they are by asking questions of the other players. Questions may only be answered by yes or no. Consider these: Do I like to be touched? Am I a place you have intercourse? Am I exposed in public? Do I wish I were larger? Smaller? Do I get waxed?

After about thirty minutes, players announce who they think they are.

stuff

| | PROPS: Pair of dice | PLAYERS: Foursome or more |

A roll of the dice determines what task each player must perform. Roll a six and you become Sex Master of the circle. The longer you drink—er, play—the better this game gets.

Sit in a circle on the floor with a glass of wine or your beverage of choice. The host takes a sip and rolls the dice first, then passes the dice to the right. The game continues, with each player taking one turn and passing the dice to the right, for as long as you like. **rolls are as follows:**

2 Kiss the guest of your choice anywhere except on the lips.

3 Pantomime three sexual positions (cannot repeat what has been done before).

4 Nibble someone's ear for thirty seconds, player's choice.

5 Ooops, you're the sex slave! Crawl around the circle and freshen players' drinks while complimenting them on their bodies.

6 Congratulations, you are the Sex Master, you lucky thing you. For one turn, the Sex Master has ultimate power. The Sex Master can rearrange the seating order of the circle,

make any two people make out (excluding her or himself), demand to see one person's nude body part, or issue any other devious command he or she can dream up. The Sex Master must be obeyed or the infidel is banished from the circle for one round.

7 Kiss the person to the right of you while the person to the left of you takes a drink.

8 Tell a naughty joke or, if you don't know one, describe a sexual experience.

9 Remove a piece of clothing.

10 Spend twenty seconds playing with the hair, or head, of the person two people to the right of you.

11 Kiss the person to the left of you while the person to the right of you takes a drink.

12 Tickle the person two people to the left of you for fifteen seconds.

in the clo

PROPS:	PLAYERS:
Closet or dark room, a deck of cards	Foursome, preferably more

This version of Seven Minutes in Heaven pairs you with random partners, but just what happens in those seven minutes is entirely up to you.

 Shuffle and then fan out a deck of cards on the table. Each player chooses one card.

 The player drawing the low card must go to a closet or a secluded room that is pitch black.

 The remaining players each draw another card. This time, the high card must join the low card in the closet or room for seven minutes (one of the remaining players keeps time). Anything or nothing can happen; it's totally up to the players in the dark.

 When time is called, the first player comes out of the dark, but the second player stays. Everyone draws again, and the high card goes into the dark to join the other player for seven minutes.

 The game continues until everyone has paired once.

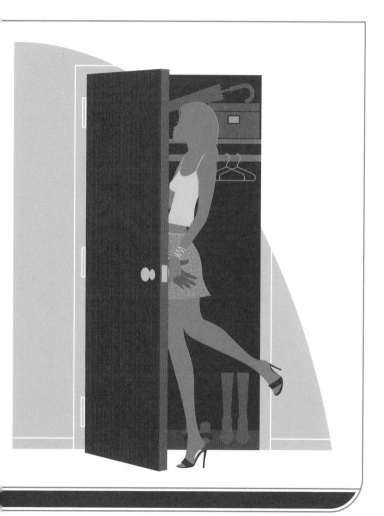

truth or dare

PROPS:	PLAYERS:
Nothing but guts	Threesome or more

We've revamped this classic from childhood to really get the heart racing. Will you choose to tell the truth or perform a dare? The beauty of this game is that you can play it anywhere—at a bar, at a party, on a plane. In fact, different locations inspire entirely different types of dares.

 The first player asks of any player, "Truth or dare?" The selected player must respond with what he or she would rather do: answer a question truthfully or act on a dare. Players take turns challenging other players, going clockwise around the circle.

 Make the questions as intimate as you dare, and the dares as wild as you can think of. This game could go from Hot Stuff to Hardcore if you want it to.

 A successfully completed dare is worth 20 points, and an honestly answered question (you be the judge) counts for 15 points. A player may decline to answer a question or to act on a dare, but the person is docked 10 points.

 The first player to score 100 points wins.

dirty scrabble

	PROPS:	PLAYERS:
★	Scrabble game	Threesome or foursome

Did you know that Scrabble means "to grope frantically"? It's true. With that in mind, this board game practically begs for a dirty version. So dust off that Scrabble board, put on your naughty thinking cap, and grab a dictionary (or perhaps a porn magazine would be more useful).

 Set up and play the game according to the regular Scrabble rules.

 Players should try to spell out words with sexual meanings or sexual connotations. Think dirty.

 Rather than playing for the highest score, the player with the most dirty words wins, and he or she gets a crack at the big prize, which is chosen by other players and spelled out with Scrabble tiles. The tiles are shaken or scrambled and spilled onto the board. The winner has sixty seconds to unscramble the phrase or word. If he or she does it in time, the player gets the prize. Some suggestions: Body Massage, Shower with Us.

flash in

Remember Spin the Bottle? The first time you played it as a kid might have been the first time you kissed someone in a provocative way, and it still works as a tried-and-true naughty party staple. But we've spiced it up a bit here. Remember how you once got to spin again if a girl got a girl or a boy got a boy? Now there is a price to pay for refusal. As the flashlight spins, more is revealed as the game goes on!

 Sit in a circle in the dark. Make sure it is pitch black. Place a flashlight in the middle and switch it on.

 The first player spins the flashlight. Whomever the beam lands on has the choice: he or she must either kiss the person who spun the flashlight or remove a piece of clothing. The flashlight is turned off for either the kiss or the clothing removal.

 The person who was chosen by the flashlight becomes the next person to spin it. When the player is ready, he or she turns the flashlight back on and takes a turn. Once a person is completely naked, his or her only choice is to kiss the spinner.

the dark

frisk!

Everyone knows your sense of touch is heightened when you are blindfolded. This game puts your fingers to the test.

Play music that rocks the crowd and serve a cocktail to loosen inhibitions. One player is chosen to be blindfolded first. Once he or she is blindfolded, the other players don extra clothes or jackets, or trade clothes between one another, and then stand in a line.

The blindfolded player is guided to the start of the line. Start the timer and signal the player to begin.

The blindfolded player must feel each guest until he or she can correctly identify the person. The blindfolded player continues along the line until all players have been frisked and correctly identified.

Each player gets a turn to be blindfolded. The winner is the one who takes the shortest amount of time to identify all the players. As an added incentive, the winner gets to blindfold the player of his or her choice and enjoy a two-minute session of no-holds-barred touching.

wet kiss

PROPS:
Ice cubes, a timer or watch

PLAYERS:
Foursome or more

Crank up the icemakers. This game will raise the temperature of guests as ice cubes are passed, mouth to mouth, until they melt into a kiss. Of course, if you're serving ice, you'll need drinks to go with it.

 Serve guests fragrant drinks on the rocks such as mint juleps, preferably outside on a hot, sunny day.

 After the first round of drinks, seat guests in a circle. The first player, chosen at random, takes a large, fresh ice cube and puts it in his or her mouth. The player may hold the ice cube in his or her mouth as long as possible, but no longer than thirty seconds, before passing it to the person to the right.

 The ice cube keeps getting passed around the circle until it melts completely. Whoever's mouth the ice cube melts in wins and can choose to kiss anyone in the circle. Crawl over and French kiss with icy tongues. Pop in another ice cube and start the game again.

naughty

PROPS:	PLAYERS:
None	Five or more

★

Sardines is the opposite of Hide and Seek—one person hides and everyone else seeks. As seekers find the hider, they all squeeze into the hiding place together. When you're packed in like sardines, what else can you do but make the most of it? This game is best played in a large house or yard, or park.

Choose one person to be "It." Give the player five minutes to hide before the rest of the group disperses to find him or her.

The first player who finds the hider must make out with, or at a minimum maintain full body contact with, the hider until a second finder comes along. Then the second finder must join the other two, making out (and/or maintaining full body contact) with the others. Each new finder must join the group in a similar fashion.

The last one to happen upon the hider/finders is the loser and is It for the next round.

sardines

big apple

PROPS:	PLAYERS:
Fresh apples, washed and cored	Foursome or more

Take a bite of a big apple and you might just end up in someone's mouth. It's always fun to start this game with a round of sour apple martinis.

 All players sit in a circle.

 One player begins by biting into a previously cored apple and, with apple still in teeth, passes it to the person on the left. This person must take the apple in his or her teeth, pass it to the next person without dropping it, and take a bite as it's passed.

 The player who consumes the apple so that there is nothing left to pass wins, and he or she gets to choose whose lips he or she likes the most. Together they get "seven minutes in heaven."

bad simon

PROPS:	PLAYERS:
None	Foursome or more

The game Simon Says is all about power, control, and obedience—who says it's just for kids? Better listen up to what Bad Simon says!

 Choose one person to be Bad Simon, and position other players in front of Bad Simon.

 Bad Simon calls out an action, sexual in nature, for all to follow, such as, "Play with yourselves," "Take off your shirts," "Shake your booty," "Moan," or "Come up and kiss me all over!!" But the player must preface each command with "Bad Simon Says." If Bad Simon does not say this, and another player follows the command, that player is out of that round. If a player refuses to do as Simon says, he or she is out of that round.

 The last person standing in line is the winner and gets to be Bad Simon in the next round.

booty

Flip all your tiddlywinks into the cup and get the best prize of all: a flash of the other players' assets. Choose a different body part to reveal at each round: tits, genitals, or ass! If you can't find regular tiddlywinks, you can use poker chips instead.

Each player sets out their six tiddlywinks equidistant from the cup in the middle of the table. The object is to flip them one at a time into the cup.

The first player flips a tiddlywink with the flipper. If the disc lands in the cup, the player continues until he or she misses. Once the player misses, the turn passes to the next player. If a tiddlywink is covered by another player's on the table, it can't be moved until the one on top is flipped by its owner.

The first player to get all his or her tiddlywinks in the bowl wins. Each loser must flash the requested body part to the winner.

winks

sock it

Your mother always told you to wear clean socks, and that's about the only clean aspect of this game.

Each player is given a number, and this number is written on a piece of paper, folded, and placed in a hat or bowl.

Players remove shoes and sit in a large circle, socks on.

One player picks two numbers at random from the bowl. Those two people go into the center of the circle and each tries to get one of the other person's socks off before the other player gets his or hers.

Once one person wins, both players rejoin the circle and two new numbers are picked at random. These players go into the center of the circle to sock wrestle, and so on. Once a player loses both socks, he or she is out for that round.

The last person with at least one sock on wins. If the player has one sock, he or she can demand that any two players (excluding him or herself) engage in a fifteen-second passionate kisses. The circle decides whether the kiss is passion-

to me

ate enough, and if not, they have to try again. If the winning player has two socks on at the end, the player *also* gets a passionate, fifteen-second kiss with any other player.

naked polo

PROPS:	PLAYERS:
Swimming pool	Foursome or more

Maybe it's just me, but Marco Polo always seemed like just a socially acceptable way for adolescents to get in a few quick gropes. This version dispenses with the pretense of acceptability and gets players wet, naked, and fondling in no time. Don't try this at the public pool.

 Choose one player to be "It." That player must keep his or her eyes closed at all times—no peeking! All other players must be either in the pool or have some part of their body in the pool at all times.

 When the player who is It says "naked," the others must shout "polo," but they are allowed to move around as much as they want. The person who is It tries to tag the other players. Once tagged, that person must remove his or her bathing suit and becomes It.

 If the tagged person is already naked, he or she must be briefly fondled by the tagger before becoming It. The last person with his or her bathing suit on wins and gets to choose one player to personally remove his or her suit and engage in a full sixty seconds of mutual fondling in the water.

the
spank

PROPS:	PLAYERS:
Dictionary	Twosome or more

If you ever fantasized about your teacher, this is the game for you. Naughty girls and boys who don't do their homework get their pants and panties yanked down for a spanking.

Choose who will play the teacher and who will play the student(s).

The teacher asks one student to spell a sex word out loud, spelling bee style. Some stumpers might be: cunnilingus, fellatio, voyeurism, dominatrix, ben-wah balls, and phallic.

If the student makes a mistake, the teacher pulls his or her pants down and spanks the student.

After ten words, roles are reversed until everyone's had a chance to be teacher. In this game, whether you win or lose depends on your predilections.

RAUNCHY

naked twister

We've bent the rules of this classic children's game so that someone's clothes are sure to come off. Pssst—the key to winning is to keep your opponent on one side of the sheet so that he or she has to go under or over you to reach most of the circles.

 Get barefoot.

 Spread the vinyl Twister mat on the floor. Players stand at opposite ends, with the spinner positioned in the center. Each takes a turn spinning and then moving the designated body part to the color on the mat.

 You lose a round if you fall or your elbow or knee touches the sheet. The loser removes a piece of clothing before continuing on to the next round. The first one completely naked loses the game.

RAUNCHY

bag o'

PROPS:
Blindfold, two bags, and six props for each player

PLAYERS:
Twosome

Both players experience pleasure during this game, as each tries to fool the other with the most unusual touch sensations he or she has ever felt. Play this game as naked as you dare to be.

1 Each person collects six different items with which to massage his or her partner and places them in a paper bag.

2 Have one partner stretch out comfortably on a flat surface and put on a blindfold.

3 The other partner pulls out items one by one and massages, tickles, and touches various parts of the other person's body as he or she tries to guess what it is. The blindfolded person can roll over to feel sensations on the back as well as the front.

4 For each correct guess, the blindfolded partner scores a point.

5 After the six items have been used, change places and let the other partner try out his or her own bag of tricks.

6 The partner with the highest score wins.

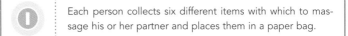 RAUNCHY

five-card

PROPS:	PLAYERS:
A deck of cards	Foursome, or up to seven

Here's a saucy take on that old poker classic—Five-Card Stud. Each time you lose, you lose a piece of clothing.

 Start with a full deck of cards and fully clothed players.

 Follow the rules of Five-Card Stud (see page 122). However, for each hand all players who do not fold bet one item of clothing. Raising is allowed.

 The losing hands take off however many pieces of clothing they bet. The winner takes off nothing and may put back on one piece of clothing even if he or she raised more. He or she also collects the pot of winnings!

 As players become completely naked, they lose and are out of the game. Keep playing until only one player has clothes on—and becomes the winner.

RAUNCHY

strip

butt=naked croquet

Who said croquet has to be a stodgy old game played at outdoor tea parties? Lose the whites and turn this into a naughty garden game. Turn to page 124 for information on how to play croquet. It's also festive to serve gin and tonics with lime—a traditional English cocktail.

 Place the wickets on the lawn according to traditional rules.

 Split into two teams of two: red and yellow balls against blue and black. The object of the game is to get your team's balls through all the wickets, in order, and hit the peg in the center of the court. The balls must go through each wicket twice, once in each direction.

 However, players get to have a little naughty fun along the way. Each time a team knocks a ball through a wicket, they get to tell the other team which item of clothing to remove.

 The first team, naked or clothed, who hits the center peg after going through all the wickets twice wins.

 The losing team runs two laps around the croquet field and refills everyone's drinks.

nasty bl

PROPS:
Deck of cards, a whip or
paddle, a table or counter

PLAYERS:
Foursome or more

All dressed up in spikes and leather with no place to go? Deal this game of blackjack and the party will come to you. All players at this party must wear black lace or black leather, and a bottle of Jack Daniels wouldn't hurt.

1 Select one person to be the dominatrix dealer. This is an important role, as the dealer is also the spanker and holds the whip or paddle.

2 Rules follow the traditional game of Blackjack (see page 123). When asking for another card, say "spank me, please" instead of "hit me" (though "hit me" works, too!).

3 If a player loses, he or she must remove a piece of clothing and get a spanking from the dealer. If a player wins, he or she can put a piece of clothing back on; if a player wins and is already fully clothed, he or she gets to spank the dealer. If a player loses and is already totally naked, the dealer can increase the severity of punishment at his or her discretion. If a dealer and player tie (called a "push"), then nothing happens.

4 The dealer must remove an item of clothing each time he or she busts (goes over 21). If the dealer draws a blackjack, the dealer gets to put a piece of clothing back on. When the dealer is naked, the round ends and a new dealer is chosen.

ride my

PROPS:	PLAYERS:
Music, a riding crop or paddle	Eight or more players

Remember after-school riding lessons? Those britches were positively sexy. You don't need to be an upper-crust socialite to enjoy the bouncy ride. Just grab a riding crop, if you have one, and hang on to your mount. If no crop is available, then use a paddle, and put some bad-ass music on to get those ponies rared up.

 Players strip to their underwear.

 For each round, a new player is chosen to be the Riding Master. Of the remaining guests about half are the horses and half are riders, but make sure there is one less horse than riders.

 The "horses" get down on all fours and form a straight line. The riders form a circle around them.

 When the Riding Master cues the music, the riders gallop in a circle around the horses.

 At the Master's discretion, the music is stopped, at which point the horses can start to gallop and the riders must try to mount them. One rider will be left horseless, and he or she receives a spanking with the crop from the Master. Down with those undies, bend over, and take your punishment— you're out of the game.

RAUNCHY

pony

6

The Riding Master pulls out a horse from the lineup and the music starts again. The one horse and rider remaining at the end of the game wins.

biig bad

PROPS:	PLAYERS:
None	Foursome or more

Here's an adult version of the Wolf and the Easter Eggs where players choose sexual positions instead of colors for the Wolf to guess. This is best played in a large house or backyard.

1 Choose one player to be the Big Bad Wolf, who must stay in a lair at the opposite end of the room or space until the chase begins.

2 The remaining players huddle together, and each player chooses the name of a sexual position.

3 The Wolf calls out a sexual position. If he or she guesses yours, you must run a predetermined obstacle course through the house or area and back to the safety of the huddle before the Wolf catches you. (For example: from the living room to the kitchen to the dining room and back.)

4 If you are caught, the Wolf takes a piece of your clothing back to the lair and you are out of that round.

WOLF

5 The last player remaining wins and gets to be the new Big Bad Wolf. All the other players are now part of the huddle, but they cannot put back on clothes that are in the wolf's lair. Play continues until everyone is naked.

baby, will tongue

PROPS:	PLAYERS:
None	Foursome or more

A variation on Honey, If You Love Me, Smile, this version will have guests smiling much sooner! The object is to get one player to make another player smile by asking a dirty question.

 Players sit in a circle, and one player begins the game.

 Standing in the middle of the circle, he or she randomly approaches guests asking, "Baby, will you tongue me?" The player can make as many funny or lewd faces as he or she wants.

 The other player must answer with a straight face, "Yes, I will tongue you, but I just can't smile." If the player smiles, he or she must remove a piece of clothing, then change places and ask the question. If the player doesn't smile, the player asking the question must approach someone else. If no one smiles, the asker must remove an item of clothing and try again.

RAUNCHY

you
me?

4 When there is only one player left who has not been in the middle, the game is over. That last player gets to choose anyone else to French kiss for as long as he or she wants— or make it a Hardcore game, if you wish.

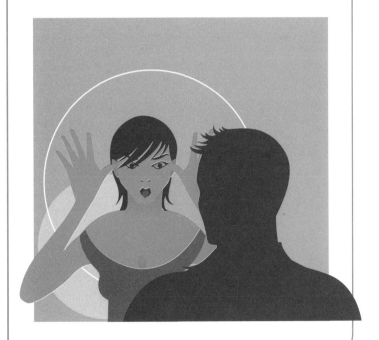

paddles

PROPS:
a ping-pong table, or a
long table; twelve glasses,
two ping-pong balls,
and two paddles

PLAYERS:
Twosome or more

Most every kid played ping-pong, but here's a naughtier way to make use of those paddles . . . if you have the balls.

Divide into two teams, with one team at either end of the table. Arrange six glasses, filled with your beverages of choice, at each end in a triangular pattern: one glass in the front, two glasses side by side just behind, and three in a row across the back.

The object of the game is to get your ball into the other team's glasses after bouncing the ball once on the table. Each time your ball lands in an opponent's glass, you score a point, and the opponent removes the glass from the table and drinks the contents.

The first team to wipe out the opponent's six glasses wins that round, and the losing team must drop their pants or panties and be paddled by the winning team.

Teams continue playing till a team scores 24 and wins the game. The winning team gets to watch the losing team perform a sixty-second striptease for their enjoyment.

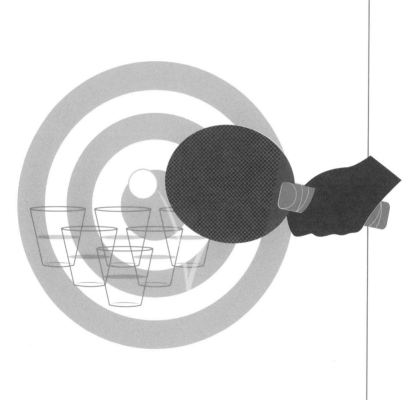

hard

tic tac blow

PROPS:
Nine shot glasses, sipping-quality tequila, paper and pen

PLAYERS:
Twosome

Sometimes the simplest game can be the most steamy. Sip each drink, don't gulp the whole thing, or you may find it's "One tequila, two tequila, three tequila, floor!" before you've finished the game.

 Draw a large tic tac toe grid on paper. Place a shot glass half-filled with tequila on each of the nine squares.

 Each player takes a turn, one plays X, the other O. You must lift the shot glass and drink (only some, not all) before marking the spot.

 As in the traditional game, the first to get three in a row wins. The best out of five games wins and the loser must blow the winner on the spot, or else perform some other sexual favor on demand. If you play to a tie three times in a row, both players must blow each other at the same time.

Note: If you'll be playing several rounds of this game, try pouring different drinks in the shot glasses: tequila in three glasses, sangrita (a spicy blend of tomato, orange juice, and chiles) in another three, and a lime drink in the remaining three. Mix them up on the board and enjoy!

HARDCORE

wicked

PROPS:	PLAYERS:
A pair of dice, tape, pen	Twosome or more

Couples who need a nudge to go beyond their comfort zone will find this game offers risks worth taking. Prepare to explore your partner's wicked side!

Tape over all sides of a pair of dice except for the one dot. On one die, write one sexual act (such as kiss, lick, bite, suck, tweak) on each taped-over face. On the other die, write an erogenous zone of the body on each taped face. So you'll have five actions on one die and five body parts on another.

Each player takes a turn throwing the wicked dice and must perform whatever the dice say on the other player. For instance Kiss/Lips or Lick/Neck. If playing with a group, the person rolling the dice gets to choose who to perform the act on.

If you roll snake eyes, you can perform any act stated on the dice, and you get to roll a second time as well. But, alas, if you roll a dot on the dice and a body part or action on the other, you lose your turn.

porn rum

PROPS:	PLAYERS:
Deck of cards, paper, pen	Twosome

Do you know your partner's wildest dreams? Would you be willing to turn them into reality? That's what's at stake with this naughty gin rummy game! I highly recommend playing this game over brunch to start Sunday off with a bang. To loosen inhibitions, make a couple of mimosas or French 75s (shake gin, cointreau, and lemon juice together and add champagne). If you have time, it would be sporting to play twice so each partner has a chance to win.

① Each person writes down one thing he or she has always wanted the other person to do (perhaps "spank me hard," "spend a full hour on steamy foreplay," "walk out to get the morning paper in the nude," and so on). Do not show your partner the paper yet. Just sip your drink and smile.

② Shuffle a deck of playing cards and play a traditional game of Gin Rummy (see page 121 for rules).

③ The first one to score 100 points wins. The winner gets to read his or her secret desire out loud, and it must be fulfilled by the loser.

alphabet

PROPS:	PLAYERS:
Paper and pen	Twosome

Remember how hard it was learning your ABCs? This game puts your learning to the test, requiring you to lick body parts that begin with the designated letter. It's best played wearing a minimum of clothing—or none at all.

 One person starts with the letter A, licking as many places on the other person's body as he or she can think of that begin with that letter. When the player can't think of any more, each entry is written down, and a point is given for each, before moving on to the next letter and player.

 The next player licks as many places on the other person's body that he or she can think of that start with B, and so on through the alphabet.

 The winner is the one with the most entries. He or she gets to choose one body part that the loser must lick, erotically, for two minutes.

truths or

PROPS:	PLAYERS:
Paper and pen	Foursome or more

Does she or doesn't she? Did he or didn't he? This little game is a sneaky way to find out what others think they know about you!

 Each person writes down on a piece of paper two truths and one lie about their sexual likes and dislikes. For instance: I like to take it from behind; I do not like giving head; French kissing turns me on (only one of which is a lie).

 Each person in turn reads the three statements out loud in any order.

 The rest of the group must decide which of the three statements is the lie. If the group guesses correctly you lose. If you fool the group you win.

 In the next round, only winners play. If all players lose a particular round, those players play again. However, players cannot repeat their own descriptions. The game continues until there is only one winner.

 Once there is a winner, the rest of the group chooses one of the winner's true statements along with a player to fulfill the act with the winner on the spot.

HARDCORE

SUCK "n"

PROPS:	PLAYERS:
A single playing card	Foursome or more

This appears to be a silly, childlike game at first, but the consequences of flubbing it are ever so X-rated. The object of the game is to pass a playing card around the circle from left to right without dropping it, using only the mouth as a suction cup. No hands.

 All players sit in a circle.

 The first player places a playing card in front of his or her open mouth and sucks in to hold it. The player passes it to the next person's mouth, blowing to release the card into the next "suction cup." And so it goes around the circle.

 If someone drops the card, he or she must suck or blow the person directly opposite. The receiver gets to choose what will be sucked or blown. If players cannot agree on which one of them dropped the card, they must kiss each other.

 The game continues until there is only one person left who has not dropped the card in passing. That person "wins" and gets to be sucked or blown simultaneously by two others of his or her choice.

HARDCORE

blow

hot seat

PROPS:
A large table, a long tablecloth that reaches to the ground (a sheet will do), shot glasses, a bottle of vodka (or other liquor)

PLAYERS:
Foursome or more

Here's a naughty way to enjoy after-dinner drinks at the table. Or rather under the table. Consider this a refresher course in table etiquette . . . no laughing at the table, and mind your manners.

 Everyone takes a seat around the table, then pulls their pants and underwear down around their ankles (or hikes up their skirts), with the tablecloth covering all exposed private parts. Nothing should seem to be amiss from above the table.

 Everyone knocks back the first shot. The first one to set his or her glass back down is the first to go under the table. The person may do whatever he or she pleases to anyone. Lick a knee, caress a thigh, or . . .

 Whoever smiles first (and the entire table is watching) must down a shot and is next to go under the table.

 The longer someone spends below, the more interesting things get. Smile, you're in the hot seat!

sticky

Remember your mother admonishing that "you can't have your cake and eat it, too"? This game proves her wrong. If your guests are gourmands, you'll want homemade whipped cream, perhaps with a bit of amaretto. But good old store-bought whipped cream works just fine.

One person plays referee to the others.

The referee creates a short phrase, scrambles the letters (or the words, if the phrase is long) so it is not easily readable, and writes the jumbled phrase with an indelible marker on different pieces of paper, one for each player. Suggestions: Eat me good; Lick me harder; Suck me dry.

Place one of these papers in the bottom of the bowls, one for each player. Fill the bowls with whipped cream.

Place a bowl on the table in front of each player, who can stand or sit, but whose hands must remain behind his or her back.

When the referee shouts "Eat," players dive into the whipped cream, eating their way through until they find the

HARDCORE

paper at the bottom, which they must take out of the bowl with their lips, tongue, or teeth.

6 The first player to correctly unscramble the phrase and shout it out loud wins. The prize? The winner gets extra whipped cream placed on his or her chosen body part by the referee, to be licked off by two losers of his or her choice.

sexy cha

PROPS:
Paper and pens, two bags

PLAYERS:
Foursome or more

Here we've taken classic Charades to new lows with suggestive, silent pantomimes sure to harden the softest of body parts. Since charades originated in eighteenth-century France, pop some Champagne while you play! See page 123 for complete rules.

All players wear robes, with nothing underneath.

Agree on the number of rounds to be played. Divide guests into two teams. Each team retreats to a room to come up with sexy phrases for the opposite team to pantomime. The theme of these charades is Porn Movie Titles. If you don't know any, make them up by corrupting popular movie titles, such as *Saving Ryan's Privates*, *Field of Creams*, *Around the World in 80 Lays*, and so on. Write each phrase on a separate piece of paper and put them in a bag. The teams rejoin in the room and exchange bags.

One team begins by having a player pull a phrase from the bag. The player can sip bubbly and review the phrase for no more than fifteen seconds. The player must then take off his or her robe and pantomime the phrase in the nude; his or her team must guess the phrase in two minutes or less. A player from the opposing team plays timekeeper.

HARDCORE

4 If the team guesses the phrase correctly, the clock is stopped and the time is written down. If no one guesses correctly, the team is penalized and given a time of two minutes.

5 The player puts the robe back on, and play switches to the opposite team. The game goes back and forth between the teams until all players have performed on both teams. Play as many rounds as have been agreed to.

6 Add up the total times for each team. The winning team is the one with the least amount of time recorded.

7 The losing team must disrobe and pantomine for two minutes a sexual act described by the winning team. The scene can be directed like a porn film, with the winners being the directors.

spotlight

PROPS:	PLAYERS:
Flashlight	Foursome or more

This is a nighttime version of Hide and Seek. Can an orgy alfresco be far behind? This is best played in a large house or a very private backyard.

1 One person is the seeker and holds the flashlight, turned off.

2 The others run and hide while the seeker closes his or her eyes and counts out loud to one hundred, at which point he or she switches on the flashlight and begins searching for the others, who may be moving about and changing places.

3 When a hider is caught in the beam of light, the seeker calls out his or her name. The hider must freeze, drop his or her pants, and with the flashlight doused, let the seeker do whatever he or she wishes on the spot.

4 Once completed, the hider is the new seeker and tries to find others for a secret tryst in the dark.

HARDCORE

dildo

	PROPS: Harness, a dildo	PLAYERS: Six players or more

Button, button, who has the button? In this case, it's a harness looking for its dildo.

Choose someone to begin in the middle of the circle, wearing a harness. Ideally, the person should be naked, but the harness can be worn over pants if players wish.

The other players stand in a circle with hands behind their backs. One player has a dildo and starts passing it around the circle, but always behind the backs of the players so the person in the middle can't see who has it. Obviously, the circle has to stand very close together.

The player in the middle walks toward different people in the circle asking if he or she has the dildo. If the person doesn't have it, he or she responds by saying "cold." If it's near, or the person is holding it, he or she says "hot." All the time, the dildo is being passed behind players' backs.

The person in the middle calls out the name of the player he or she thinks has it. The person whose name is called must hold up his or her hands. If the person has the dildo, he or

dildo

she must attach it to the harness, kneel down, and suck it for fifteen seconds.

5 If the player in the middle guesses incorrectly after three times, he or she loses. The person holding the dildo becomes "It." The loser must attach the harness with the dildo onto the new player in the middle and suck the dildo for fifteen seconds before rejoining the circle. The game continues.

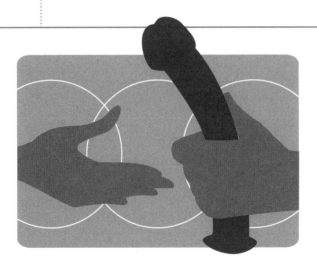

hot p

PROPS:	PLAYERS:
Vibrator with batteries	Foursome or more

Here's a great way to get everyone a-buzz.

1 One person is in charge of the music while the others form a circle, one holding the vibrator, which must be turned on.

2 When the music starts, the players pass the vibrator around as if it were a hot potato.

3 When the music stops, whoever is holding the vibrator must pull down his or her pants and perform a fifteen-second massage. The player in charge of the music keeps time and starts the music up after the fifteen-second show.

4 The vibrator continues around in this manner, the music starting and stopping at will. The first one to come wins.

down, do

	PROPS: Tennis ball	PLAYERS: Threesome or more

Inspired by a child's game from the land down under, this version of Down, Down, Down is for adults who want to really get down.

 Begin by throwing a tennis ball back and forth at random among the players.

 The first time someone drops or misses catching a ball directed at him or her, the person must get down on one knee, continuing to play.

 The second time someone misses the ball, the person must get down on both knees.

 The third time the person misses, he or she must crawl around the circle and give everyone thirty seconds of pleasure before departing the circle. If players wish, they may choose to pleasure only the opposite sex.

 The last one in the circle must be pleasured by his or her player of choice.

HARDCORE

appendix

RULES FOR CLASSIC

GAMEſ

GIN RUMMY

Deal ten cards to each player. Place the remaining deck in the center.
Organize your hand into "melds," that is, sets of three or four cards of the
same value, such as three aces or sequential numbers of the same suite
(such as 5, 6, and 7 of hearts). Face cards are worth 10 points, aces are
worth 1, and number cards are worth their number value. To begin a turn,
draw a card from either the top of the deck or the discard pile. Discard
one card from your hand for each new card taken so that you always hold
ten cards. Alternate turns around the circle. The object is to get rid of the
"deadwood" in your hand so all your cards form melds. When this happens, a player calls "gin" out loud and wins the hand, scoring 25 points,
plus the total number of points from the cards in the player's hand.
Winner of the game is the first one to score 100 (or 200, or whatever total
is agreed upon).

FIVE-CARD STUD

This is a simple game of poker. Cards are ranked high to low in the following order: Ace, King, Queen, Jack, and number cards 10 down to 2. Aces are always high. The suits (clubs, spades, hearts, diamonds) are all of equal value. Each player is dealt five cards face down, one at a time, beginning on the dealer's left. Place the remainder of the deck in the middle of the table. The first player to the dealer's left begins: he or she can place a bet and after the betting round is complete, can draw up to four new cards, discarding an equal number so there are always five cards in hand. A player can "stand" by drawing no new cards.

If the first player does not wish to open betting, he or she can say "check"; players can continue "checking" in turn until one player places a bet, and then all players must match that bet to stay in the game. If you wish to match a previous bet, put down the same amount. You raise the bet by laying down the amount previously bet plus an additional bet. All players must match the raised bet to stay in. To withdraw from the game is to "fold"; you do so by turning your cards face down on the table and forfeiting your bettings. When the betting stops, all players show their cards. The player with the highest value hand wins the pot. Winning hands include, from the lowest to the highest:

- **HIGH CARD:** The player holding the highest-valued card wins. With ties, compare the second-highest card, and so on.
- **ONE PAIR:** Two cards of equal value (two 7s, for example). If other players also have a pair, the highest-valued pair wins.
- **TWO PAIR:** Two sets of pairs (two 7s and two Jacks).
- **THREE OF A KIND:** Three cards with the same value (three 7s).
- **STRAIGHT:** All five cards are in numerical sequence (6, 7, 8, 9, 10).
- **FLUSH:** All five cards are the same suit (all hearts).
- **FULL HOUSE:** Three cards of the same value, with two cards of the same value (three 7s and two 4s).

- **FOUR OF A KIND:** Four cards of the same value (four Kings).
- **STRAIGHT FLUSH:** Five cards in sequence and in the same suit (2, 3, 4, 5, 6 and all hearts).
- **ROYAL FLUSH:** The highest-valued hand is 10, J, Q, K, A, all in the same suit.

BLACKJACK

The point of this card game is to beat the dealer by accumulating cards that total or come closest to 21 without going over. Face cards count 10 points. Aces can be either 1 or 11.

Each player places a bet, then is dealt two cards face up. The dealer also gets two cards, but one is face up and the other face down. Each player, starting at the dealer's left, can ask for another card (say "hit me") or can stand with what he or she has. When all players are finished, the dealer turns over the down card: the dealer must stay on counts of 17 or higher, and must draw a card with 16 or lower.

If a player makes 21 with the first two cards dealt (a face card and an ace), that's called "blackjack" and the player automatically wins 1.5 times the bet. If a player scores a lower count than the dealer, the person loses the bet. If the player scores a higher value than the dealer, the person wins an amount equal to the bet. If a dealer and player tie, it's called a "push" and the bet remains on the table.

CHARADES

In Charades, two competing teams pantomine phrases, written by the other team, in a race against the clock. Each player has a maximum time limit of two minutes per turn. The clock stops when a team member guesses the phrase. If no one guesses in two minutes, the team is penalized by having two minutes added to its score. The team with the least amount of total minutes wins.

Start a charade by indicating whether you'll mime a movie (pretend to crank an old movie camera), a book (unfold your hands as if they were a book), or an expression (make quotation marks with fingers). For a television show, draw a square for a TV screen. Indicate the number of words in the phrase by holding up the appropriate number of fingers; indicate syllables by holding the appropriate number of fingers on your forearm. Continue to pantomime the phrase using classic "mime," such as cupping your ear for "sounds like," stretching out hands as if pulling elastic to indicate a word should be lengthened, and chopping with your hand if a word needs to be shorter.

CROQUET

Croquet is played on a rectangular lawn measuring 100 by 50 feet, or as close as you can get to that. Cut the grass short, and mark the corners of the croquet lawn with stakes or flags. Place a stake near each opposite end of the field, with two wickets directly in front. Arrange the five remaining wickets to form a double diamond pattern the length of the lawn, joining with the wickets already placed.

Two teams require four balls. One team plays with blue and black balls and the other with red and yellow. Players hit one at a time, and the order of play is blue, red, black, yellow. Each player has a mallet and strikes the ball with the end of the mallet. To help keep track of what wicket is in play, each player can use colored clips or clothespins to mark their next wicket.

The object of the game is to get your ball through all the wickets, in the proper order. Begin at one stake, through the two hoops, and follow the double diamond pattern along the right side of the field, hitting your ball through the two wickets at the opposite end and hitting the stake before returning on the opposite side of the double diamonds. Players score one point per wicket (the ball has to pass completely under the wicket and to the other side) and one point per stake (the ball must hit the stake). The winning team is the first to score 14 wicket points and 2 stake points per ball.

Players get only one shot. However, if a ball hits another ball, or if a ball hits a wicket or a stake, the player gets a bonus turn.

- **ROQUET:** When a player's ball hits another, the striker earns 2 extra shots.
- **ROVER:** Your ball becomes a rover when it has successfully completed the course. You can keep it in the game to help your team win and prevent the other team's balls from advancing. You may hit any other ball once per turn (gaining bonus shots only for hitting a ball, not for going through a wicket or hitting a stake). Any player may put a rover out of the game by hitting it into the finishing stake (although the rover's team will earn the point for hitting the stake).

If a ball goes out of bounds, it is brought back onto the lawn and placed one mallet length into the court.

AUTHOR BIOGRAPHY:

FRANCES HILL was born in Lawrence, Kansas, and is currently a resident of New York. Hill's wickedly naughty endeavors can be regularly found in the gossip columns of the city's many tabloids.

. . . .

ILLUSTRATOR BIOGRAPHY:

DAN SIPPLE left his blue-collar roots in Detroit for big-city life in Los Angeles and never looked back. His illustrations have appeared in many publications, including the *New York Times*.